Sounds All Around Us

Different Sounds

Charlotte Guillain

www.heinemannlibrary.co.uk
Visit our website to find out more information about Heinemann Library books.

To order:

☎ Phone +44 (0) 1865 888066

📄 Fax +44 (0) 1865 314091

🖥 Visit www.heinemannlibrary.co.uk

Heinemann is an imprint of Capstone Global Library Limited, a company incorporated in England and Wales having its registered office at 7 Pilgrim Street, London, EC4V 6LB – Registered company number: 6695582

"Heinemann" is a registered trademark of Pearson Education Limited, under licence to Capstone Global Library Limited

Edited by Charlotte Guillain, Rebecca Rissman, and Catherine Veitch
Designed by Joanna Hinton-Malivoire
Picture research by Tracy Cummins and Tracey Engel
Originated by Heinemann Library
Printed by South China Printing Company Limited

ISBN 978 0 431 19338 0 (hardback)
13 12 11 10 09
10 9 8 7 6 5 4 3 2 1

British Library Cataloguing in Publication Data
Guillain, Charlotte
Different sounds. - (Sounds all around us)
534
A full catalogue record for this book is available from the British Library.

Acknowledgements
The author and publishers are grateful to the following for permission to reproduce copyright material: Alamy pp. **4 top left** (©UpperCut Images), **6** (©Ted Pink), **13** (©Derek Croucher), **15** (©JUPITER IMAGES/Polka Dot), **19** (©PCL), **20** (©Alan Myers), **21** (©anna Sherwin), **23a** (©anna Sherwin), **23c** (©Ted Pink); Getty Images pp. **5** (©Donald Miralle), **7** (©Lester Lefkowitz), **10** (©Holger Leue), **11** (©AFP/BORIS HORVAT), **18** (©Niki Mareschal), **23b** (©Lester Lefkowitz); iStockphoto pp. **4 top right** (©Frank Leung), **4 bottom right** (©Peeter Viisimaa); Jupiter Images p. **14** (©Image Ideas); NASA p. **8** (©GRIN); Photolibrary pp. **12** (©David & Micha Sheldon), **16** (©Index Stock Imagery), **17** (©Picture Press/Manfred Delpho); Shutterstock pp. **4 bottom left** (©devi), **9** (©Amra Pasic).

Cover photograph of Silk Road, China reproduced with permission of Getty Images (©Keren Su). Back cover photograph of some teenage girls playing flutes reproduced with permission of Alamy (©Jupiter Images/Polka Dot).

The publishers would like to thank Nancy Harris and Adriana Scalise for their assistance in the preparation of this book.

Every effort has been made to contact copyright holders of any material reproduced in this book. Any omissions will be rectified in subsequent printings if notice is given to the publisher.

Contents

Sounds

There are many different sounds.

We hear different sounds around us every day.

Sound waves

Sounds make the air shake,
or vibrate.

sound wave

When the air vibrates, it is called a
sound wave.

Loud and quiet sounds

Some sounds are loud.

Big sound waves make loud sounds.

A drum can make loud sounds.

A trumpet can make loud sounds.

Some sounds are quiet.

Small sound waves make
quiet sounds.

A harp can make quiet sounds.

A flute can make quiet sounds.

High and low sounds

Some sounds are high.

Very fast sound waves make high sounds.

Some sounds are low.

Very slow sound waves make
low sounds.

A triangle can make high sounds.

A double bass can make low sounds.

What have you learned?

- Big sound waves make loud sounds.

- Small sound waves make quiet sounds.

- Very fast sound waves make high sounds.

- Very slow sound waves make low sounds.

Picture glossary

 **double bass** musical instrument that looks like a large violin

 **sound wave** when the air shakes very quickly

 **vibrate** shake very quickly

Index

Notes to parents and teachers
Before reading
Tell the children that sounds can be loud or quiet, high or low. Explain that big sound waves make loud sounds, and small sound waves make quiet sounds. Also explain that if sound waves are fast, they make high sounds, and if sound waves are slow, they make low sounds.

After reading
• Give the children a box of objects, including for example, a harmonica, a drum, bells, a bouncy ball, a whistle, a rattle, and anything else you can think of. Ask the children to make predictions about the types of sounds the objects will make. Tell the children to shake, blow, or bang the objects to make different sounds.
• Read *Sounds All Around* by Wendy Pfeffer.